Handling
Sickle Cell Disease

by Yvette LaPierre

Content Consultant
Tirthadipa Pradhan-Sundd, PhD
Assistant Professor
Department of Medicine
University of Pittsburgh

Handling
Health Challenges

Essential Library
An Imprint of Abdo Publishing
abdobooks.com

abdobooks.com

Published by Abdo Publishing, a division of ABDO, PO Box 398166, Minneapolis, Minnesota 55439. Copyright © 2022 by Abdo Consulting Group, Inc. International copyrights reserved in all countries. No part of this book may be reproduced in any form without written permission from the publisher. Essential Library™ is a trademark and logo of Abdo Publishing.

Printed in the United States of America, North Mankato, Minnesota.
052021
092021

THIS BOOK CONTAINS
RECYCLED MATERIALS

Cover Photo: Monkey Business Images/Shutterstock Images
Interior Photos: Monkey Business Images/Shutterstock Images, 4, 26, 29; Shutterstock Images, 7, 20, 46, 64; iStockphoto, 9, 50, 52, 88; Phonlamai Photo/Shutterstock Images, 13; Tim Vernon/Science Source, 16; Eye of Science/Science Source, 19; Red Line Editorial, 22; Aberration Films Ltd/Science Source, 32; Damir Khabirov/iStockphoto, 35; Anna Tamila/Shutterstock Images, 36; Michael Conroy/AP Images, 40–41; Saturn Stills/Science Source, 43; Dick Whipple/AP Images, 48; Biophoto Associates/Science Source, 55; Dmytro Zinkevych/Shutterstock Images, 56; Monkey Business Images/iStockphoto, 60, 86; Kateryna Kon/Shutterstock Images, 65; Spencer Grant/Science Source, 66; Evgeny Atamanenko/Shutterstock Images, 70; Life in View/Science Source, 72–73; Steve Gschmeissner/Science Source, 77; Beranger/ Science Source, 78; Syda Productions/Shutterstock Images, 80; Supavadee Butradee/Shutterstock Images, 85; Pat Greenhouse/ Boston Globe/Getty Images, 90; Jim Dowdalls/Science Source, 93; Science Picture Co/Science Source, 97

Editor: Arnold Ringstad
Series Designer: Megan Ellis

Library of Congress Control Number: 2020948176

Publisher's Cataloging-in-Publication Data

Names: LaPierre, Yvette, author.
Title: Handling sickle cell disease / by Yvette LaPierre
Description: Minneapolis, Minnesota : Abdo Publishing, 2022 | Series: Handling health challenges | Includes online resources and index.
Identifiers: ISBN 9781532194993 (lib. bdg.) | ISBN 9781098215309 (ebook)
Subjects: LCSH: Sickle cell anemia--Juvenile literature. | Sickle cell anemia--Diagnosis--Juvenile literature. | Blood--Diseases --Juvenile literature. | Therapeutics--Juvenile literature. | Diseases --Social aspects--Juvenile literature. | Health--Juvenile literature.
Classification: DDC 616.152--dc23

Contents

What Is Sickle Cell Disease?

Marcus was excited for college to start in a couple of months. He'd been accepted to the state university a few hours from his hometown and had already signed up for classes. He had a room in one of the freshman dorms and had already been assigned a roommate. He and his new roommate had texted several times over the summer, and it seemed like they had a lot in common. Both of them planned to major in business, ran track in high school, and liked to play Frisbee golf for fun. They were already making plans about what to bring for their room—Marcus would bring a microwave, and his roommate was bringing a minifridge.

Marcus was making all the usual plans for going away to college. He was buying books and other supplies for classes. He and his mom had been

Preparing for college is hard work for any teen, but sickle cell disease adds its own unique challenges.

shopping for sheets and towels for his dorm room. But there was one more important task that Marcus needed to take care of before starting college. He needed to be ready to take full responsibility for managing his sickle cell disease.

Sickle Cell Anemia or Sickle Cell Disease?

Sickle cell disease is a collective name for multiple types of blood disorders, and the most common and severe type is known as sickle cell anemia. Regardless of the type, sickle cell disease often is called sickle cell anemia because most people who have the disease deal with chronic and sometimes severe anemia. Anemia is a condition in which a person's blood doesn't have enough healthy red blood cells, which can cause weakness and fatigue. Sickle cell disease is a more accurate term for the broad category, however, because abnormal hemoglobin results in a wide variety of disorders, of which sickle cell anemia is just one.

Marcus's Diagnosis

Marcus's parents learned that he had sickle cell disease a few weeks after he was born. All states test newborns for a number of inherited diseases, including sickle cell disease, and the routine test had revealed that Marcus had the condition. As soon as their doctor contacted them, his parents immediately began reading as much as they could about the disease so that they would be ready when Marcus might

When parents learn that their child has sickle cell, they may want to do their own research to learn how to best support their child.

begin having symptoms at about five or six months old. They learned that sickle cell disease is a blood disorder that people are born with. It results in a number of symptoms and complications, including pain, infection, and organ damage. The symptoms vary from person to person and range from mild to severe, so Marcus's parents prepared themselves as best they could.

> "Don't ever look at your disease as a hindrance. You are more than capable of going to college and being successful. You just have to know yourself and pay attention to your health because you won't be able to do that unless you're at your best health-wise."[1]
>
> —*Mikeia, a college student living with sickle cell disease*

Throughout his life, Marcus and his parents worked with doctors and teachers to keep Marcus as healthy as possible. Marcus visited his doctor regularly, and his teachers and coaches knew he needed to keep well hydrated and not overexert himself. Despite all the precautions, Marcus was hospitalized numerous times for pain and missed a lot of school. He often felt like he was playing catch-up with homework and tests and worried he wouldn't get into college. But between the severe pain episodes, his life went back to normal. He hung out with friends and got caught up in school. His hard work paid off when he got his college acceptance letter, and he refused to allow sickle cell disease to come between him and his plans for the future.

Finding the right kind of doctor is an important part of managing sickle cell disease.

Taking Responsibility

With the help of his parents and doctors, Marcus began preparing to manage his health by himself. The first step was to identify doctors near campus who had experience treating sickle cell disease. He knew he needed a hematologist, or a doctor who specializes in blood disorders, and that he would be responsible for calling to make his own appointments. His parents helped him fill out the paperwork he would need to transfer his medical records and

Discovery of Sickle Cells

Sickle cell disease has likely affected people in Africa for thousands of years. It wasn't identified by the medical community in the United States, however, until 1910. That year, Chicago physician James B. Herrick published a paper in which he described some odd-shaped red blood cells. He had found them in a blood sample taken from a 20-year-old dental student from Grenada who suffered from severe anemia. He described the cells as shaped like crescents or sickles. Normal red blood cells are shaped more like doughnuts. This was the first description of what came to be known as sickle cells, and the name sickle cell anemia was coined based on Herrick's paper.

prescriptions to his new health-care center.

After so many years with the disease, Marcus had learned how to manage his symptoms at home, but he also knew when it was time to call the doctor. He knew that if his pain got so bad that he couldn't take care of it with the painkillers that his doctor had prescribed, he would need to go to the hospital for help. He also knew to go to the doctor if he ran a high temperature, because people with sickle cell disease are more at risk for infections, and the resulting fevers can trigger pain episodes.

Marcus had always known that living a healthy lifestyle was the best way to avoid complications of sickle cell disease, but in the past he'd always let his mom worry about that. Now Marcus decided to focus on it himself. He tried to make sure he got at least eight hours of sleep every night. He figured out what foods he'd need to look for at his campus dining hall once he got to school. He made sure he drank at least eight to ten glasses of water a day, and he brought water with him on his runs so that he wouldn't become dehydrated. He also joined the local chapter of the Sickle Cell Disease Association of America (SCDAA).

At the end of August, Marcus's car was packed with books, clothes, sheets, towels, and a microwave. He had everything he needed to head off to college. Most importantly, Marcus had a plan to manage his sickle cell disease and take care of himself to make sure that he could be healthy and successful.

Sickle Cell Disease Association of America

The National Association for Sickle Cell Disease was founded in 1971. In 1994, it became the Sickle Cell Disease Association of America (SCDAA). The mission of the SCDAA is to advocate for people affected by sickle cell disease and to work with community-based organizations and medical facilities to improve those people's quality of life. It provides resources and networking opportunities for those living with the disease and their families. In addition, the SCDAA raises awareness of the disease and promotes research for a universal cure.

Circulatory System

The circulatory system keeps bodies alive and healthy by delivering oxygen and nutrients to cells and removing waste. The circulatory system is made up of the heart, lungs, and blood vessels. The heart is a muscle that pumps blood through the network of arteries and veins. An average adult has five to six quarts (4.7 to 5.6 L) of blood and a system of blood vessels that would measure about 60,000 miles (96,560 km) long if the vessels were laid end to end. As blood circulates through the body, it delivers oxygen and nutrients to all the cells and picks up waste. The blood travels through the lungs, where it gets rid of waste and picks up more oxygen. Then it heads back to the heart, where it is pumped through the body again.

Sickle Cell Disease

Marcus is a fictional character, but his experiences represent what life is like for a young adult living with sickle cell disease, particularly one who is preparing to take full responsibility for his health care. Sickle cell disease encompasses a group of inherited blood disorders. That means that the disease passes from parents to children, and children who inherit the disease are born with it. Sickle cell disease is the most common inherited blood disorder in the world and affects millions of people. In the United States alone, an estimated 100,000 people live with sickle cell disease, the majority of whom are of African ancestry.[2]

Sickle cell disease causes the body to produce abnormal hemoglobin. Hemoglobin is a protein in red blood cells that carries oxygen throughout the body to tissues and organs. Normal red blood cells are round and flexible, and they move easily through blood vessels. The abnormal hemoglobin makes

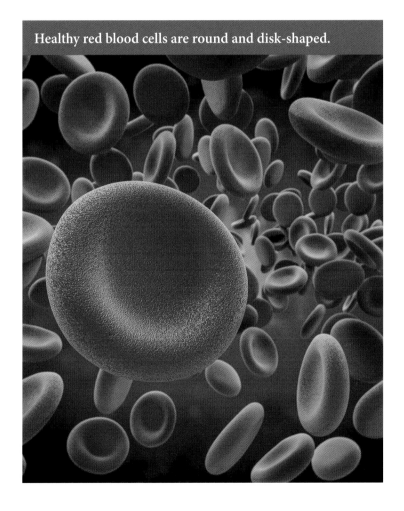

Healthy red blood cells are round and disk-shaped.

red blood cells become long and curved. The shape resembles the blade of a cutting tool called a sickle, which is how the disease got its name. The sickle cells are stiff and sticky. They tend to form clumps in blood vessels, blocking blood and oxygen from reaching parts of the body. The result can be episodes of severe pain and a host of other health problems, including frequent infections, organ damage, neurological problems, and fatigue from a lack of healthy red blood cells.

Sickle cell disease is serious and lifelong. Before the 1970s, most people living with sickle cell disease died in childhood, primarily from infection, stroke, and heart failure. Now people with sickle cell disease live on average into their mid-fifties and beyond.

"Living on Borrowed Time"

Sickle cell disease was not a well-known disease in the 1950s in the United States, despite how many people, mostly people of African descent, were living with it. For many Americans, their first introduction to the disease was an article in *Time* magazine. Marclan A. Walker, a 21-year-old West Virginia college student, published a personal account of the challenges of living with sickle cell disease in the January 1959 issue of *Ebony* magazine. *Ebony* was a magazine with a mostly Black audience. The story was then picked up by *Time*, bringing it to a wider readership. Reflecting the reduced lifespan of many people with the disease, the article's title was "Living on Borrowed Time."

Research has led to a better understanding of the disease, and better diagnosis, prevention, and treatment have prolonged the lives and improved the well-being of people living with sickle cell disease. Sickle cell disease can be cured through a blood and bone marrow transplant. Unfortunately, only a small number of people with the disease are able to have this treatment. Researchers, however, are making promising strides in their search for a universal cure and better treatments to improve the lives of all people with sickle cell disease.

"The shape of the reds was very irregular, but what especially attracted attention was the large number of thin, elongated, sickle-shaped and crescent-shaped forms."[3]

—Dr. James B. Herrick, the discoverer of sickle cells, November 1910

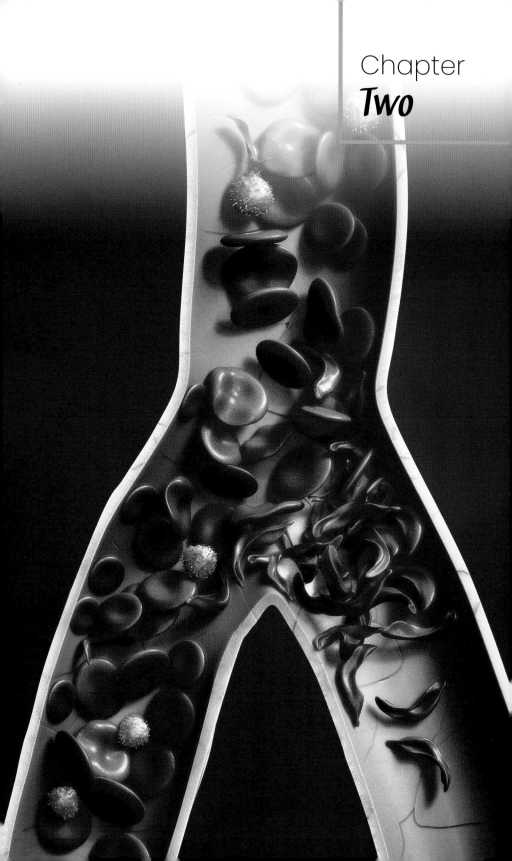

The Cause

Sickle cell is an inherited disease, and it was the first of these for which scientists identified the exact genetic cause. It is caused by a defect in the gene that helps make hemoglobin. Red blood cells with normal hemoglobin are disk-shaped and flexible. They pass easily through the smallest vessels to deliver oxygen where it is needed.

The defective gene causes the body to produce an abnormal type of hemoglobin, which is called hemoglobin S (HbS), or sickle hemoglobin. HbS reacts to low levels of oxygen in the blood by causing rigid protein strands to form within the red blood cells. These rigid strands change the shape of the cells. The cells elongate and bend, creating a shape like a banana or sickle.

These sickle-shaped cells are stiff rather than flexible, making it difficult for them to flow through blood vessels. In addition, they tend to clump up

Sickle-shaped red blood cells can block the flow of blood, leading to the symptoms of sickle cell disease.

and stick to vessel walls, which creates dams of cells that slow or stop the flow of blood. When blood stops flowing, so does oxygen, which creates problems in the body. And the less oxygen in the blood, the more HbS forms sickle-shaped red blood cells. This creates a cycle that continues to cause harm.

Complications

Blocked blood vessels in the arms, legs, chest, or abdomen can cause episodes of severe pain. Repeatedly blocked blood vessels can lead to tissue and organ damage. Many people with sickle cell disease eventually develop severe kidney, lung, liver, and brain damage.

Children with sickle cell disease are prone to infections and are at increased risk for strokes. In addition, sickle blood cells only survive about one-tenth as long as normal red blood cells. This constant shortage of red blood cells results in anemia. Anemia is a lack of red blood cells that results in fatigue and weakness.

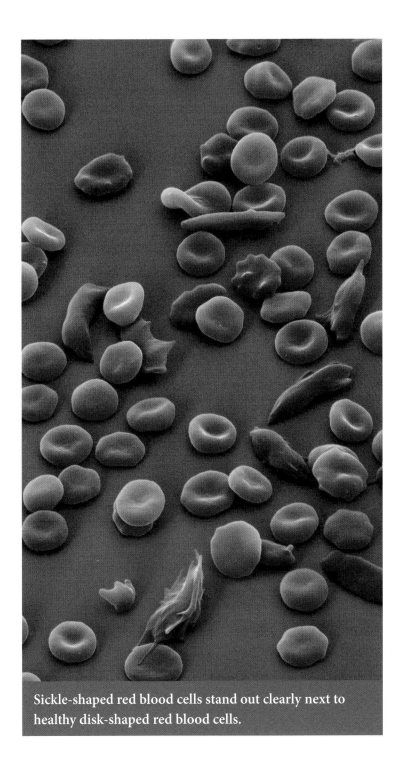

Sickle-shaped red blood cells stand out clearly next to healthy disk-shaped red blood cells.

Leg pain is one typical symptom of sickle cell disease.

Inheriting Sickle Cell Disease

All babies inherit one hemoglobin gene from each parent, giving them a total of two. Most children inherit two normal copies of the gene that tells the body how to make hemoglobin. Two normal genes, called hemoglobin A genes, instruct the body to produce normal hemoglobin protein. Some adults, however, carry a flawed, or mutated, form of the hemoglobin gene. If a child inherits two flawed copies, he or she will have sickle cell disease. Children who inherit a normal gene from one parent and an abnormal gene from the other parent are said to have sickle cell trait.

People who have sickle cell trait carry the mutated gene and can pass it on to their children, but they generally do not have pain episodes or other signs of the disease. When both parents have sickle cell trait, each child they have has a one in four chance of inheriting sickle cell disease.

First Molecular Disease

Throughout his career, chemist Dr. Linus Pauling was interested in the relationship between chemistry and the body and focused his research on the hemoglobin molecule. In 1949, he proved for the first time that a human disease—sickle cell disease—was caused by an abnormal protein molecule. He recognized that the abnormal hemoglobin protein was the result of a genetic mutation inherited from both parents. He and his coauthors coined the term *molecular disease* in a paper on the discovery. Since then, many other diseases have been classified as molecular, or arising from a single molecule, including muscular dystrophy and Alzheimer's disease.

Inheriting Sickle Cell Disease

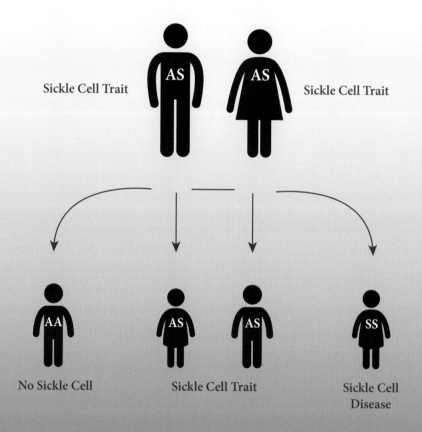

Sickle Cell Trait AS   AS Sickle Cell Trait

AA
No Sickle Cell

AS   AS
Sickle Cell Trait

SS
Sickle Cell
Disease

This diagram shows the chances of passing the sickle cell gene from parents to children. If each parent has one normal and one abnormal hemoglobin gene, there is a one-in-four, or 25 percent, chance of inheriting two normal hemoglobin genes (AA). In this case, the child would not have sickle cell disease or sickle cell trait. There also is a 25 percent chance of inheriting two hemoglobin S genes (SS), and this child would have sickle cell disease. Each child has a 50 percent chance of inheriting one normal and one sickle hemoglobin gene (AS), or having sickle cell trait. No matter how many children the couple has, each child has the same odds of inheritance. In other words, if the first child is born with sickle cell disease (SS), the second child has the same 25 percent chance of being born with the disease.

Types of Sickle Cell Disease

There is more than one type of abnormal hemoglobin gene. Different combinations of these genes result in different types of sickle cell disease. The most common type is HbS, which produces the sickle-shaped red blood cells. Children who inherit two HbS genes have a type of sickle cell disease known as sickle cell anemia. This is the most common and often most severe form of sickle

Sickle Cell Trait

People who have sickle cell trait, or just one copy of an abnormal hemoglobin gene, are known as carriers. This means that they can pass the abnormal gene to their children but generally don't have symptoms of the disease themselves. People with sickle cell trait, however, must still be careful. At extreme altitude or when very dehydrated, a steep drop in blood oxygen levels can result in some problems related to sickle cell, including shortness of breath and severe pain episodes. People with sickle cell trait must be cautious about such activities as flying in airplanes, mountain climbing, and scuba diving. People with sickle cell trait can have trouble with muscle breakdown or heat stroke during intense physical activity. It's important, therefore, for people with sickle cell trait to stay hydrated and not get overheated or overtired. In a few cases, sickle cell trait has been linked to a rare kidney cancer. However, it is not clear whether the effects on people with sickle cell trait are caused by this trait or by other associated mutations. More research is needed to discover the cause of these problems.

cell disease. Other mutated forms of hemoglobin genes include hemoglobin beta-thalassemia, hemoglobin C, hemoglobin D, and hemoglobin E.

Some forms are named for the regions in which they are typically found, including D-Punjab and O-Arab. Sickle cell

Genes and Mutations

Genes are pieces of DNA that contain the information for making a specific protein, and they are passed from parents to children. These proteins create muscles, bones, blood, and everything else that makes bodies function properly. A mutation is a permanent change in the DNA sequence that makes up a gene; it is kind of like a typo in a set of instructions. That change can disrupt how proteins are made, which can contribute to disease. A hereditary mutation, such as HbS, is inherited from a parent and is present from birth throughout the person's life. Every baby receives DNA from both parents. If the DNA has a mutation, the child will have that mutation in all of his or her cells.

Another type of mutation, called acquired mutation, is not present at birth. The mutation happens during a person's life and is caused by an environmental factor, such as too much sun. Acquired mutations are only present in some cells, not every cell of the body, and they cannot be passed on to children.

beta-thalassemia, in which a child inherits HbS and hemoglobin beta-thalassemia, and hemoglobin SC, in which a child inherits HbS and hemoglobin C, are two other fairly common types of sickle cell disease. The disease types hemoglobin SD and hemoglobin SE are much less common. The severity of sickle cell disease varies based on the type a person has, and it also varies across individual cases of the disease.

The First Mutation

For many years, scientists believed that the mutation that causes sickle cell disease showed up many times in many different populations of people. In 2018, however, scientists traced the sickle cell mutation back to a single baby born in West Africa 7,300 years ago. Scientists made this discovery after analyzing the genomes, or complete sets of genes, of almost 3,000 people.[3] The mutation would have given that child a better chance of surviving malaria and living long enough to have children, some of whom also inherited the mutation. More than 250 generations later, that one child's mutation is continuing to provide descendants with protection against malaria, as well as creating problems for many others. This genetic discovery can help scientists better understand sickle cell disease.

Sickle Cell Demographics

Sickle cell disease affects millions of people throughout the world. According to the World Health Organization (WHO), more than 300,000 babies are born each year with a form of the disease, and approximately 5 percent of the world's population carries the genes for hemoglobin disorders, mostly for sickle cell disease.[1] Sickle cell disease can be found in almost any place in the world. However, it is most prevalent in sub-Saharan Africa. In some sections of Africa, the prevalence of sickle cell trait is as high as 30 percent.[2] It is also relatively common in other tropical regions, such as South and Central America and the Caribbean. Thalassemia types of the disease are most common in Asia, the Middle East, and Mediterranean countries, including Turkey, Greece, and Italy.

Sickle cell disease is most common among people of African descent, but it can affect those of any race or ethnicity.

The Malaria Connection

The parts of the world where sickle cell disease and sickle cell trait are most common are the same areas where malaria is prevalent. Malaria is a disease caused by a parasite carried by mosquitoes. When a mosquito bites a person, it can transfer the parasite. The parasite then invades healthy red blood cells, making the person sick. Malaria kills about 1.2 million people per year in Africa, Asia, the Middle East, and other tropical areas.[4] Beginning in the 1940s in Africa, doctors noticed that patients who had sickle cell disease were more likely to survive malaria than those without the disease. In 1954, doctors discovered that sickle cell trait protected people from malaria. Sickle cell trait results in some sickled cells, though generally not enough to cause problems. When the spleen destroys the abnormal sickle cells, it destroys the malaria parasite too. Researchers now believe that the sickle cell gene evolved as a defense against malaria.

US Prevalence

The US Centers for Disease Control and Prevention (CDC) report that approximately 100,000 people in the United States live with sickle cell disease, making it the most common genetic disease in the country. Furthermore, about 2.5 million people in the United States carry the sickle cell trait.[3] The people most at risk for sickle cell disease are those with a family history of sickle cell disease or sickle cell trait. Another risk factor is ancestry. In the United States,

Sickle cell disease is commonly passed from generation to generation within a family.

most people who have sickle cell disease are those whose ancestors came from areas of the world where sickle cell disease is most prevalent, particularly Africa. About one in every 365 Black babies born in the United States has sickle cell disease, and about one in 13 is born with sickle cell trait.[5]

People in the United States with a Hispanic heritage also are at an increased risk. About one in 100 Hispanic Americans is born with sickle cell trait.[6] It is important to note, however, that people of all races and ethnic groups can have sickle cell disease

Race and Health Care

Some in the health-care community believe that sickle cell disease has not received the attention and research money it deserves. A 2013 study highlights this perspective. The study found that cystic fibrosis, another inherited disease, received as much as 11 times more research funding than sickle cell disease, even though the condition affects less than one-third the number of people in the United States that sickle cell disease does. Some note that one main difference between the two inherited diseases is that sickle cell patients are mostly Black or from another minority group, and cystic fibrosis patients are not. Race, they conclude, may be a factor in funding decisions. "I don't know if that's the sole reason" for the difference in funding, says Reginald French, president and CEO of the Sickle Cell Foundation of Tennessee, "but I do believe that's a top contributing factor."[7]

or sickle cell trait. The rate of sickle cell trait among white people in the United States is estimated at about half the rate for Hispanics, and the rate among Asian Americans is slightly lower than that. All babies in the United States, regardless of their risk factors, are tested for sickle cell disease.

Tracking Sickle Cell Disease

The CDC and participating states have been gathering data on sickle cell disease since 2010 in order to help researchers and health-care providers improve the health of those with the disease. The CDC gathers data from various sources, including newborn screening records, medical charts, and health-related data sets such as statistics on emergency room visits. Hematology labs, facilities

"If someone with sickle cell disease goes to an urban hospital, and you're an urban African American male, and people just look at you like, 'Yeah, right, you just want these meds,' it's instant stress (for the patient). Even when seeking help, when people are in helping professions, there's raised eyebrows and skepticism. There is, 'No, we don't believe you. Prove you have sickle cell disease.'"[8]

—Dr. Lewis Hsu, pediatric hematologist

Hematology labs are among the sources of data that health authorities use to track and study sickle cell disease.

that study blood samples, help generate useful data as well. By studying all this data over time, the CDC hopes to determine how the number of people with sickle cell is changing.

The CDC also is studying whether prevalence varies by region in the United States. For example, an analysis of data found that 4,689 Californians had sickle cell disease in 2016. Of those, 1 in 3 lived in Los Angeles County.[9]

The data help identify trends in diagnosis, treatment, and health care, which can be used to create new policies and health-care changes to benefit those with sickle cell disease. For example, the CDC can use data to develop maps to show where people with sickle cell disease live and where the closest health-care

A New Health Strategy

In 1971, President Richard Nixon proposed a National Health Strategy. The strategy recognized that not all people in the United States have the same access to health care. The strategy focused, in part, on the need to expand sickle cell research. In his special message to Congress, President Nixon wrote: "It is a sad and shameful fact that the causes of this disease have been largely neglected throughout our history. We cannot rewrite this record of neglect, but we can reverse it. To this end, this administration is increasing its budget for research and treatment of sickle-cell anemia."[10] Funding increased in the following years, and life expectancy for people with sickle cell disease rose.

centers are. These maps can help people with sickle cell disease get better care.

Economic Costs

Sickle cell disease has significant economic impacts on the health-care industry and the economy. According to the CDC, the medical costs for a child with sickle cell disease averaged between $11,702 and $14,772 during 2005, and about 40 percent of these children had at least one hospital stay.[11]

The CDC found that in California, people with sickle cell disease went to the emergency room an

Longer Lives

In the United States, newborn screening for inherited diseases that started in the 1970s, as well as the introduction of a pneumonia vaccine in 2000, have resulted in a dramatic rise in life expectancy for people living with sickle cell disease. Before 1986, the life expectancy was 14 years of age on average. Many children died as a result of pneumonia infections. Now children diagnosed with sickle cell disease receive vaccinations and antibiotics early to prevent pneumonia. Between 1986 and 2002, the mortality rates for people with sickle cell disease dropped by 68 percent for ages zero to three, 39 percent for ages four to nine, and 24 percent for ages ten to 14. Better medications and treatments, such as routine blood transfusions, also have increased life expectancies.[12] In 2019, a study estimated the life expectancy of sickle cell patients at 54 years.[13]

Steep medical bills can increase stress for people with sickle cell disease or parents of children with the disease.

average of three times a year from their late teens until their mid-fifties. The high medical costs associated with living with sickle cell disease impact the individual's and the family's personal finances. In addition, insurance companies and health-care systems assume a share of the costs, which can impact the overall economy and the availability of medical resources. A 2018 study found that the total economic burden of sickle cell disease is approximately $3 billion per year in the United States.[14]

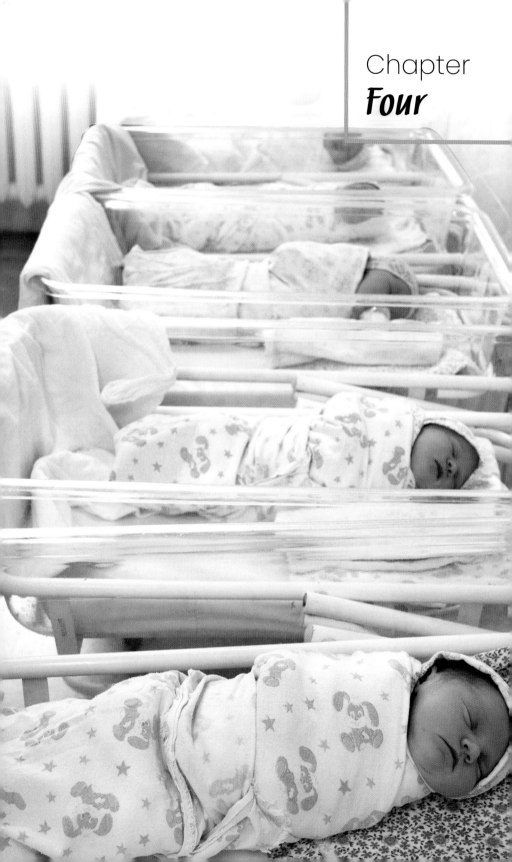

Diagnosing Sickle Cell Disease

If a person has sickle cell disease, it is present at birth. Most babies, however, don't show any symptoms until they are five or six months old. The number and severity of symptoms varies from person to person, so some babies will have symptoms early on, and others might not develop symptoms until months later.

One of the first signs or symptoms of sickle cell disease is often painful swelling of the hands and feet, usually accompanied by a fever. The swelling is the result of sickle cells getting stuck in blood vessels and blocking the flow of blood into and out of the hands and feet.

Babies are typically screened for sickle cell and other inherited diseases soon after birth.

Fetal Hemoglobin

Babies' bodies make fetal hemoglobin in the womb and for several months after birth. Like adult hemoglobin, fetal hemoglobin binds to oxygen and carries the oxygen into and out of cells. Fetal hemoglobin, however, binds to oxygen more strongly than adult hemoglobin to enable the transfer of oxygen from the mother to the fetus. Since fetal hemoglobin does a better job of keeping cells oxygenated, it protects against sickle cell disease. Once fetal hemoglobin is replaced with adult hemoglobin at about five or six months of age, the cells begin to sickle. Some people with sickle cell disease also have a genetic mutation that allows them to continue making fetal hemoglobin throughout their lives, which protects them against complications of sickle cell disease. Researchers may be able to use this knowledge to create a new treatment or cure for sickle cell disease that involves reactivating fetal hemoglobin in adults.

Jaundice is another early sign. This is yellowing of the skin or yellowing of the whites of the eyes, also known as icterus. It occurs when lots of red blood cells break down at once, which is one of the complications of sickle cell disease. Babies with sickle cell disease may be fussy or lethargic due to anemia, a very common complication of sickle cell.

Newborn Screening

People who are concerned that they may have sickle cell disease or sickle cell trait can be diagnosed with a simple blood test that detects the abnormal hemoglobin protein. Most diagnoses of sickle cell disease, however, are made as a result of routine newborn screening for a number of inherited and treatable conditions. The conditions that newborns are screened for differ from state to state, but all 50 states and the District of Columbia mandate screening for sickle cell disease as part of their standard newborn screening programs.

"I was about 3 years old when I started presenting with pain in my wrists and ankles."[1]

—Mimi, a person living with sickle cell disease

History of Newborn Screening

Newborn screening is a public health service in the United States designed to identify babies who are at increased risk for developing certain diseases. It began in the 1960s when doctor Robert Guthrie developed a blood test that could detect whether newborns had a metabolic disorder called phenylketonuria. In 1973, scientists developed a screening method for sickle cell disease. In 1975, New York became the first state to require newborn screening for sickle cell disease. Today all states and the District of Columbia require newborn screening for sickle cell disease, and screening tests are currently available for more than 60 other disorders. Newborn screening cannot confirm a diagnosis, so follow-up testing is always needed to determine if the disease is definitely present.

Multiple small blood samples are collected from newborns to test for a variety of conditions.

Newborn screening is done at the hospital following the birth of a baby. Within 48 hours of birth, health-care workers take a sample of blood from a newborn by pricking the heel. The sample, called a blood spot, is placed on a special type of paper and sent to a qualified laboratory for analysis. If a condition is detected, the parents and primary care doctor are notified immediately for follow-up testing. A laboratory process called electrophoresis can confirm the diagnosis of sickle cell disease.

The goal of newborn screening is to identify affected babies quickly so that they can begin treatment that will protect them as best as possible against negative outcomes. All babies born in the United States are screened unless the parent or parents choose not to allow screening for personal reasons. Currently, nearly 4 million babies born

Final Screen

Right

☐ Pass
☐ Refer

✓ No

5/11/16

reening

5/11
100

Time 1315

Foot 100

☐ Did Not Pass

Time

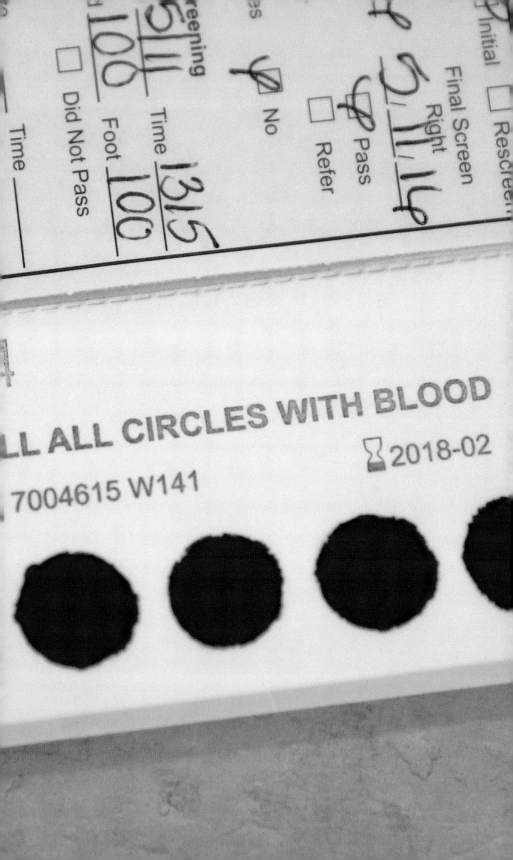

LL ALL CIRCLES WITH BLOOD

⧗ 2018-02

7004615 W141

Electrophoresis

Electrophoresis is a laboratory method that uses an electrical field to confirm the presence of sickle cells. First, red blood cells are separated from the hemoglobin and put on special paper or gel. Each end of the paper or gel has a charge; one end has a positive charge, and the other end has a negative charge. Each form of hemoglobin, whether normal or one of the abnormal forms, has a specific electrical charge. If a cell has a strong negative charge, for example, it will be pulled far toward the positively charged end of the paper. Different forms of hemoglobin move at different rates and to different locations on the paper based on their electrical charge. The paper is divided into bands that correspond with the different types of hemoglobin. Once the test is complete, the number of cells on the band that corresponds with sickle cells helps the physician determine whether sickle cells are present and the severity of the disease. The more cells in the band, the more severe the disease.

in the United States are screened each year for sickle cell and other diseases.[2]

Genetic Testing

Babies can be tested for sickle cell disease or sickle cell trait even before they are born. Researchers use a method called amniocentesis to sample amniotic fluid, the fluid surrounding a fetus, for the abnormal hemoglobin gene. This type of test is typically done between 16 and 18 weeks in the pregnancy. It carries a small risk of miscarriage. The test can be done as an outpatient procedure, and results are generally available within a few weeks. Testing the amniotic fluid can also reveal other genetic disorders in addition to sickle cell, including cystic fibrosis and Tay Sachs disease.

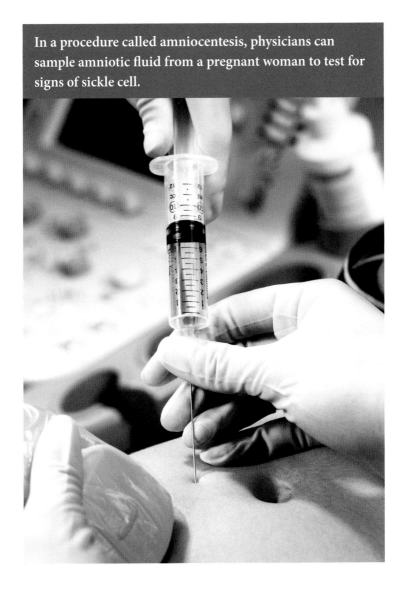

In a procedure called amniocentesis, physicians can sample amniotic fluid from a pregnant woman to test for signs of sickle cell.

Scientists also can sample the tissue from the placenta, the temporary organ in a mother's uterus that supports a developing fetus. This procedure is known as chorionic villus sampling. It is generally done around week nine or ten of a pregnancy. The risk of miscarriage is slightly higher than with the amniotic fluid test. As with the amniotic fluid test, it is an outpatient procedure. Results usually come back within a week or two.

In addition, couples in a known risk group for sickle cell disease who are planning to have children may choose to have genetic testing to determine if one or both parents carry the trait for sickle cell. Couples then meet with a genetic counselor. This is a professional with expertise in both the science of genetics and the skills involved in counseling people on personal decisions. The genetic counselor explains the risk their offspring have for being born with sickle cell disease or sickle cell trait and answers questions the couple may have. Ensuring that couples are well-informed about these risks may help reduce the rate of sickle cell births.

Sickle cell disease's effects are serious and lifelong. An early diagnosis of sickle cell disease gives parents and health-care providers the best chance to provide necessary care to a child with the disease. As medical technology has advanced, doctors have been able to make the diagnosis earlier and earlier, improving outcomes for those with sickle cell.

Quick Screening

Newborn screening in the United States is very successful in identifying children with sickle cell disease. The screening process requires laboratory equipment, trained professionals, the ability to transport blood, and reliable electricity. Unfortunately, these conditions aren't always available in the parts of Africa where the majority of sickle cell disease cases are found. In addition, newborn screening in Africa is too expensive for many families, and it can take months for the results to come back. A test that underwent study in 2018, however, may help with these challenges. The rapid result test uses simple test strips that can detect abnormal hemoglobin with just a few steps, returning a result within minutes. Easy and quick screening may save thousands of lives.

Chapter
Five

Pain Crises

Sickle cell disease can cause episodes of acute and severe pain. These are known medically as vaso-occlusive crises, but most people call them sickle cell episodes or pain crises. People with sickle cell disease may have trouble describing the pain, but they often use adjectives such as sharp, intense, stabbing, and throbbing.

The pain from a crisis is most commonly felt in the chest, abdomen, lower back, hips, and legs. It often begins at night, and an episode can last from a few hours to days or even weeks. Pain is the most common complication of sickle cell disease, and it is the main reason why people with sickle cell disease go to the emergency room or are admitted to the hospital.

Severe nighttime pain is a hallmark symptom of sickle cell disease.

What Causes a Pain Crisis?

A pain crisis can begin without warning. It starts when oxygen levels in the body drop. This drop in oxygen causes blood vessel walls to narrow. In addition, the lack of oxygen causes

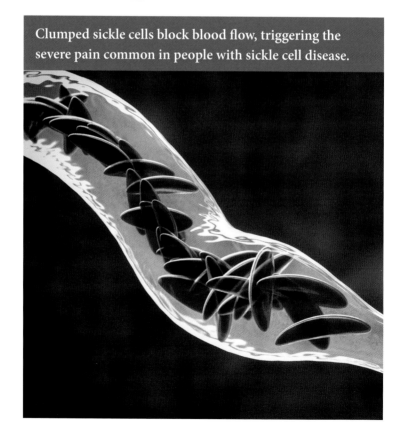

Clumped sickle cells block blood flow, triggering the severe pain common in people with sickle cell disease.

red blood cells to become sickle shaped. All blood vessel walls have a protein called thrombospondin that is sticky. In healthy blood systems, this protein is useful because it helps blood to clot after a cut or injury. But for people with sickle cell disease, thrombospondin causes the sickle cells to stick together in clumps. The combination of narrowed blood vessels and sticky clumps of sickle cells leads to blocked vessels. These blockages of cells stab into vessel walls and stop normal red blood cells from getting through and carrying oxygen to the body, causing the pain crisis. Scientists first described pain crises and their cause in 1934.

Red Blood Cells

Blood is made up of plasma, red blood cells, white blood cells, and platelets. Red blood cells, which also are called erythrocytes, contain hemoglobin. Hemoglobin is what gives blood its red color. Hemoglobin binds with the gases oxygen and carbon dioxide. Oxygen is essential for humans to live. It is taken into the lungs from the air people breathe. Red blood cells pick up oxygen as blood passes through the lungs. As blood circulates through the body, it exchanges oxygen for carbon dioxide in the cells. Too much carbon dioxide in cells is not healthy. So blood circulates back to the lungs, where the carbon dioxide is exhaled and more oxygen is picked up. Without enough healthy red blood cells, the body is deprived of oxygen, and carbon dioxide can build to toxic levels.

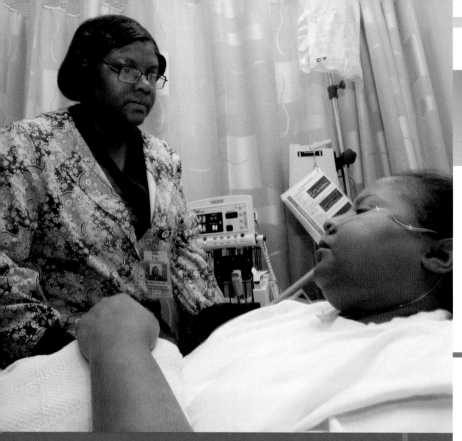

Severe pain may require a person to be hospitalized.

Pain Triggers

Many things can cause oxygen levels to drop, triggering a pain crisis. One trigger is exposure to extreme temperatures, either hot or cold. A fever can cause the body's temperature to rise quickly, which is one reason why fevers are considered a medical emergency for anyone with sickle cell disease.

Stress and exhaustion can trigger a pain crisis, as can dehydration. People with sickle cell disease must make sure they drink enough water to stay well hydrated. When exercising or staying active, people with sickle cell disease should take breaks as needed and continue drinking water. It's also important to get plenty of sleep.

The use of alcohol, caffeine, and nicotine can all trigger pain crises. Drinking too much caffeine and alcohol can result in dehydration. Alcohol abuse can increase organ damage and other health problems that sickle cell disease already causes. Research shows, too, that smoking is associated with increased risk of problems with blood flow in the lungs. Other triggers include infection, high altitude, and changes in the acidity, or pH levels, of the blood and body.

Acidosis

Blood pH, or the measure of acid and alkaline in the blood, can contribute to a pain crisis. The human body functions best at a blood pH of 7.4. If blood pH is higher, the patient has alkalosis, meaning the blood is too alkaline. If blood pH is lower, the patient has acidosis, meaning the blood is too acidic. Acidosis can trigger a pain crisis.

Diseases, and particularly kidney disease, can lead to acidosis. But many other things can cause a temporary rise in the acid levels of blood, including what people eat and drink. Not drinking enough fluids or drinking too many sugary or caffeinated drinks can contribute to changes in blood pH, as can eating too many sugary foods or not eating enough fresh fruits and vegetables. Feeling stressed, taking certain medications, and smoking tobacco or marijuana also can lead to acidosis.

Over-the-counter pain relievers, such as ibuprofen, are typically the first line of defense when a pain crisis strikes.

Treating Pain

Managing pain is the number one priority during a pain crisis. The standard treatment is to first take over-the-counter nonsteroidal anti-inflammatory drugs (NSAIDs) and drink lots of water. NSAIDs are medications such as ibuprofen and acetaminophen that reduce pain, fever, or inflammation. If that doesn't limit the pain to a manageable level, the next step is to take safe levels of stronger painkillers that the person may have been prescribed by a doctor. Some people find pain relief from nonmedical interventions, including massage, meditation, and warming pads. People with sickle cell disease work with their doctors to develop pain plans that work for them.

If people experiencing a crisis can't control the pain at home, they must go to the hospital or

Pain Dismissed

Describing the pain of a sickle cell episode can be difficult because it is unlike any pain that a person without the disease has endured. Carlton Haywood Jr., a professor at the Johns Hopkins School of Medicine who has the disease, says, "I tell people to try to imagine the worst pain they've ever been in, from a broken limb or a migraine, and then try to multiply that."[2] Unfortunately, people living with sickle cell disease report that others disbelieve them or think they are exaggerating their pain. Even worse, that includes some doctors and nurses in emergency departments. Some doctors may even worry that the person is exaggerating pain in an effort to obtain opioid painkillers. As a result, some patients going through a pain crisis must wait in excruciating pain before receiving treatment. Organizations devoted to sickle cell disease research, treatment, and prevention work to better educate health-care workers to recognize the signs and symptoms of sickle cell disease.

> "Our mission is to get our patients out of the hospital and out there living their lives. When they're stuck in the hospital, they're in pain. They lose their jobs. They miss their kids growing up."[3]
>
> —Ilene Friedman, MD, Northwell Health's Long Island Jewish Medical Center

emergency room to receive stronger medicines and intravenous (IV) fluids. This may be done on an outpatient basis, though for more severe or longer crises, the person may be admitted to the hospital. Many patients with sickle cell disease report that health-care workers don't always understand what is causing the pain or recognize the level of pain the patient is in, which can result in a frustrating and painful wait for relief.

Long-Term Effects

Repeated pain episodes over a lifetime can add up to long-term effects. Each time severe blockages occur, the body is deprived of the oxygen it needs to function properly. Without enough oxygen, the brain cannot send proper messages to the rest of the body, and muscles can weaken. Many of the body's organs can't perform their jobs without sufficient oxygen. The heart does not pump as well, and the lungs can't expand and contract properly, which makes it harder for the body to get oxygen and clear carbon dioxide. If the kidneys and liver aren't working at healthy levels they cannot metabolize needed nutrients or clear toxins from the body. Decreased oxygen levels over time break down the bones, tissues, and cartilage of larger joints, such as hips and shoulders. All this can lead to ongoing pain, organ failure, and disease.

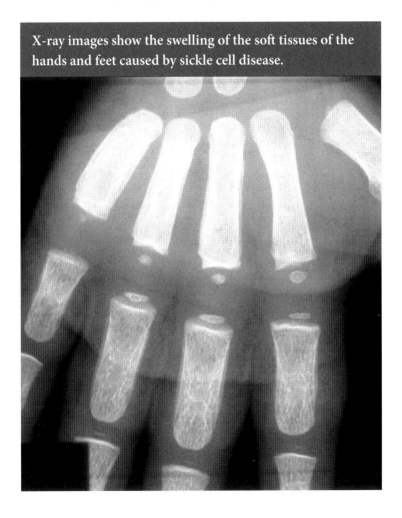

X-ray images show the swelling of the soft tissues of the hands and feet caused by sickle cell disease.

Sickle Cell Disease and Health

Most people with sickle cell disease do not have pain between crises, but some do suffer from chronic pain. In addition to pain, sickle cell disease can lead to a number of complications, which vary in type and severity depending on the individual. Some of the more common complications include anemia, infection, acute chest syndrome, and stroke.

Anemia

Anemia is a very common complication of sickle cell disease, which explains why another common name for the disease is sickle cell anemia. Because sickle cells are long and stiff, they cannot change shape easily like normal, flexible red blood cells do.

Anemia, a condition that includes fatigue, is among the usual complications of sickle cell disease.

As a result, they tend to burst and die, lasting on average ten to 20 days. Normal red blood cells, by comparison, live about 90 to 120 days.[1]

The body is constantly making new red blood cells to replace the old cells, but for a person with sickle cell disease, the body can have trouble keeping up with how fast red blood cells are destroyed. As a result, people with sickle cell disease often have anemia. People with anemia do not have enough oxygen-rich blood, causing fatigue, shortness of breath, dizziness, headaches, or an irregular heartbeat. Children with sickle cell disease may

Severe Anemia

People with sickle cell disease generally deal with mild to moderate anemia. However, sometimes anemia can be severe or life-threatening, particularly in a newborn or child. There are two main causes for episodes of severe anemia in children. The first is called aplastic crisis. It can be the result of a viral infection called fifth disease, also known as slapped cheek syndrome due to the facial rash it causes. Fifth disease is a common infection in children. However, it is dangerous for people with sickle cell disease because it can cause their bone marrow to shut down production of new red blood cells, leading to aplastic crisis. The other cause is splenic sequestration crisis, which is when sickle cells trap red blood cells in the spleen. As a result, few red blood cells are available to circulate in the body. Both cause a temporary sharp reduction in red blood cells in the bloodstream, resulting in severe anemia.

grow more slowly and reach puberty later than their peers as a result of anemia.

Infection

People with sickle cell disease are at increased risk for frequent and often severe infections. For many years the most common causes of death in children with sickle cell disease were pneumonia and other bacterial infections. Other common infections for people with sickle cell disease include meningitis, an infection of the brain and spinal cord, and hepatitis, an infection of the liver. It is strongly recommended that people with sickle cell disease receive appropriate vaccinations and seek medical attention if they develop a fever. Sickle cell

Anemia and Iron

Many people with anemia take iron supplements to manage their condition. That's because iron-deficiency anemia is the most common type of anemia. The body needs iron to make hemoglobin. Without adequate iron, the blood lacks enough hemoglobin to carry oxygen. The symptoms are similar to the anemia associated with sickle cell disease: fatigue, weakness, shortness of breath, and dizziness. Taking iron supplements can improve or cure the anemia.

That treatment will not help people with anemia caused by sickle cell disease. Sickle cell anemia is not caused by lack of iron; it is caused by a lack of red blood cells due to sickled cells. In fact, taking iron supplements can be harmful for a person with sickle cell disease because an excess of iron in the body can damage organs.

Sickle cell can leave a person more vulnerable to common infections.

disease can weaken the immune system and damage the spleen, both of which increase the risk of infection.

Common viral and bacterial illnesses, such as influenza and colds, can quickly become dangerous for a person with sickle cell disease if they lead to high fever or infection. The best defense against infections is to take simple steps to prevent infectious diseases. One simple step is making sure to wash hands frequently.

Acute Chest Syndrome

Clumps of sickle cells can block blood flow in and out of the lungs. When this happens, lung tissue is damaged and the lungs can't exchange oxygen properly. The result is a condition called acute

"Pain is the most common complication of [sickle cell], and the number 1 reason that people with [sickle cell] go to the emergency room or hospital."[2]

–CDC

The Spleen

The spleen is a small organ that filters blood and destroys old blood cells. It helps protect people from infection by removing bacteria from the blood. For people with sickle cell disease, the spleen works extra hard to replace the short-lived sickle cells. However, the spleen can be damaged so that it's not able to remove harmful bacteria. The damage occurs when sickle cells block blood flow through the spleen, leading to an enlarged and painful spleen. It can get swollen enough to be felt on the left side of the belly. Some children with sickle cell disease must have their spleens removed. Most adults with sickle cell have a nonfunctional spleen.

chest syndrome. This means at least one segment of the lung is damaged.

Acute chest syndrome often starts a few days after a pain crisis begins, and it can be accompanied by an infection. Symptoms of acute chest syndrome include chest pain, cough, and fever. The condition is serious and should be treated by a physician right away.

Stroke

According to the CDC, about 10 percent of children with sickle cell disease will have a stroke.[3] Stroke occurs when sickle cells get stuck and stop or reduce the flow of blood in vessels or arteries leading to the brain. The brain is then deprived of adequate blood and oxygen, which can cause a stroke.

"Children with sickle cell disease have an 11 percent risk of developing stroke by age 20 years."[4]

—Fenwick T. Nichols III and Steven R. Levine, authors of an article on sickle cell disease and stroke

Some people with sickle cell disease suffer a clinical stroke, which means that they exhibit symptoms of stroke. Signs of a stroke include sudden onset of weakness, dizziness, headaches, or changes to vision. Others have a silent stroke, which means that they don't have any outward signs of stroke. Silent strokes, however, still cause injury to the brain and may lead to difficulties learning, making decisions, or holding down a job. Damage from silent strokes can be detected by a type of medical imaging called magnetic resonance imaging (MRI).

Additional Complications

Sticky sickle cells can injure the blood vessels in the eye, causing vision problems. The part of the eye most commonly damaged is the retina. The retina is a light-sensitive layer of tissue that lines the inside of the eye. The retina sends visual messages from the optic nerve to the brain. When sickle cells block blood vessels leading to the retina, the vessels can swell or bleed. This, in turn, can cause the retina to detach, or lift away from its normal position. A detached retina can lead to vision loss or blindness.

Some people with sickle cell disease can develop

Priapism

Males with sickle cell disease may have unwanted and long-lasting erections that are painful. This condition, called priapism, happens when blood flow out of the penis is blocked by sickle cells. Some can find relief by urinating to empty the bladder, exercising lightly, and drinking lots of fluids. Priapism that lasts more than four hours is a medical emergency because it can do lasting damage.

Blocked blood flow leads to a wide variety of symptoms, including joint pain.

complications with their bones and joints. Sickle cells often block blood flow to large bones and joints, such as those in the legs and hips. As the flow of blood and oxygen decreases to the hips, the joints are damaged. Shoulder joints, knees, and ankles also can sustain damage. People with joint damage have pain and difficulty moving. If the condition persists and is serious, a joint replacement may be required.

Gallstones are a common problem for people living with sickle cell disease. When red blood cells break down, they release the hemoglobin they contain. The body then breaks down the hemoglobin, which releases a substance called bilirubin. Bilirubin can form stones that get stuck in the gallbladder, a small organ under the liver. A gallstone can range in size from a grain of sand to a golf ball. Gallstones can result in pain, an upset stomach, and vomiting. If gallstones persist, the patient may have to have the gallbladder removed.

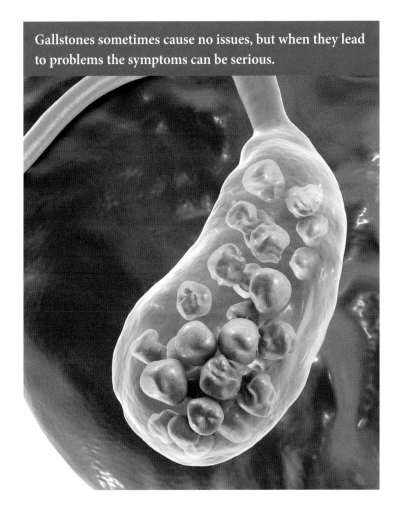

Gallstones sometimes cause no issues, but when they lead to problems the symptoms can be serious.

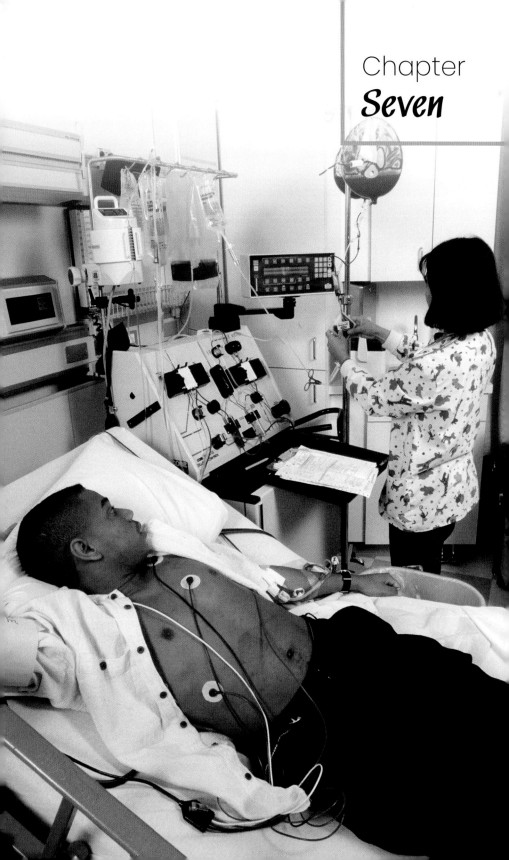

Treatment and Management

Sickle cell disease is a serious lifelong condition, but early diagnosis, regular medical care, and treatments to manage and prevent complications can reduce symptoms and lead to a longer and more active life. Because sickle cell disease is complex, people living with the disease should assemble a health-care team with physicians who know a lot about the disease and can help prevent complications. A good choice for the team is a hematologist. Patients should visit their regular doctor every three to 12 months, depending on their age and the severity of their symptoms and complications.

Doctors will recommend and monitor that their patients are receiving routine vaccinations, including those for meningitis, pneumonia, and influenza. Many children with sickle cell disease also are

Doctors have developed sophisticated ways to treat and manage sickle cell disease.

prescribed daily doses of antibiotics. All of these prevent possible infections and illnesses that can lead to more serious complications.

People with sickle cell disease may find that not all physicians and emergency room doctors are familiar with the disease. A CDC study found that, in general, family physicians see few patients with sickle cell disease. More than half of the physicians surveyed didn't have any patients with sickle cell disease in their practice, and fewer than 25 percent had five or more patients with sickle cell disease. Of the doctors who responded to the survey, only about one in five reported feeling comfortable treating a patient with sickle cell disease.[1]

It's very important, therefore, for patients to take an active role in managing their own plan of care. The first step is being as informed and knowledgeable as possible about the disease, possible complications, medications, and treatment options. One recommendation is for patients to create a notebook or binder in which they organize all materials related to their care. The binder could include doctor contact information, a schedule of medical appointments, prescriptions for medications, test results, and vaccine and immunization records. Patients can then bring the notebook to any doctor or emergency room visit. Armed with all the right information, people with sickle cell can work with the doctors on their medical team and advocate for the best possible care.

Doctor Visit

People living with sickle cell often go to the doctor's office or emergency room for treatment for an immediate problem, such as unmanageable pain or severe anemia. It's important, too, for people living with sickle cell disease to visit their doctor regularly for checkups and preventative care. Regular doctor visits can help prevent some serious problems. A regular visit to the doctor will include a number of examinations, tests, and perhaps referrals to other health-care professionals.

Penicillin Saves Lives

In 1986, a study of children with sickle cell disease showed that daily doses of the antibiotic penicillin could prevent the incidence of pneumonia infection by 84 percent.[2] At that time, pneumonia was a major cause of death in children with sickle cell disease and contributed to the low average lifespan of 14 years. In 2020, children with sickle cell disease were prescribed preventative antibiotics from three months old to five years of age or longer. Daily penicillin has not only extended the lives of people with sickle cell disease, but it also has made early diagnosis critical so that treatment can begin right away.

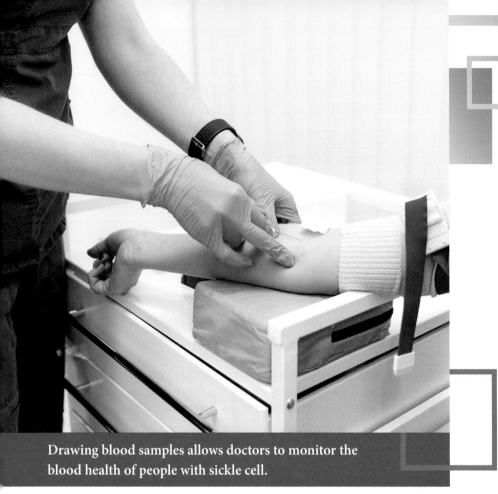

Drawing blood samples allows doctors to monitor the blood health of people with sickle cell.

The doctor will measure the height and weight of children to ensure that they are developing properly. The doctor may order a blood test to check for other health problems and a urine test to screen for kidney problems. Other tests can measure how much oxygen the blood is carrying and check to make sure the patient doesn't have too much iron, which can happen from blood transfusions. A blood transfusion is a medical procedure that puts donated blood into the body through a narrow tube placed in a vein in the arm. The body doesn't naturally remove iron from the blood, and too much iron in the body can damage the heart, liver, and other organs.

The doctor will also evaluate the health of bones, joints, and muscles. If necessary, the doctor may refer the patient to a physical therapist. The doctor may order a cognitive screen. This is a test that measures the patient's ability to think clearly, remember things, and learn effectively. Cognitive tests can reveal problems caused by silent strokes, which may not be obvious. Because stroke in children is such a dangerous complication of sickle cell disease, doctors use ultrasound machines to identify children at higher risk for stroke. Additionally, doctors recommend regular eye exams to screen for eye problems related to sickle cell disease.

Doctors will also review records to ensure that vaccinations and immunizations are up-to-date and order more if necessary. Some clinics have sickle cell educators available to talk with patients and their families and provide them with additional information about treatment options. Depending on the needs of the patient and family, a referral to a social worker may be needed to provide the patient and family with additional support.

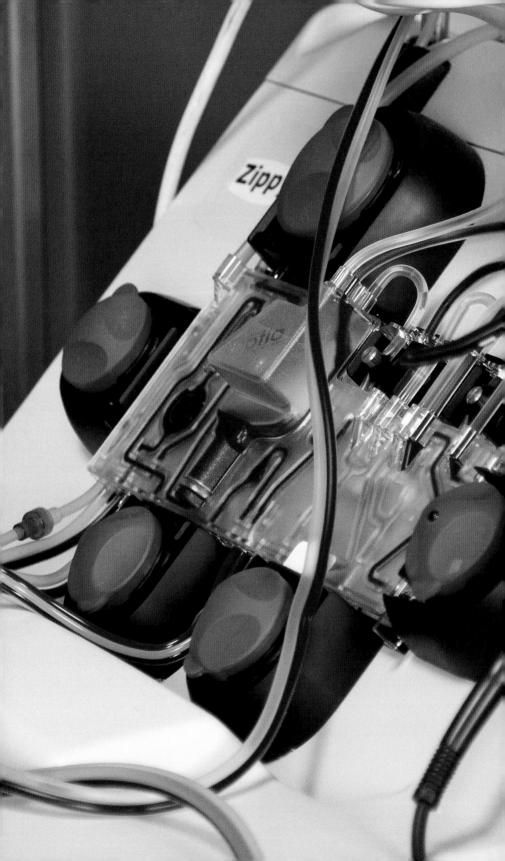

Complex machines are used to carry out red blood cell exchange therapy.

Transfusions

Everyone needs sufficient red blood cells coursing through their bodies to be healthy. One of the effects of sickle cell disease is a severe reduction of red blood cells. Many patients require blood transfusions to increase the number of healthy red blood cells in the body. A blood transfusion is a medical procedure that adds donated blood to the body through a narrow tube placed in a vein in the arm. Several types of blood transfusions are used to treat patients with sickle cell disease.

Ongoing, or regularly scheduled, blood transfusions are required by people who have previously suffered a stroke in order to reduce the chances of another one. Ongoing transfusions also may be needed by patients who don't respond well to other sickle cell disease medications and treatments. Periodic blood transfusions in children who are at high risk for stroke can reduce their risk of having a first stroke by 90 percent.[3] Acute transfusions are used to treat episodes of severe anemia in order to quickly raise the amount of red blood cells. An acute transfusion also may be needed in cases of stroke, acute chest syndrome, and multiple organ failure caused by sickle cell disease. Another treatment, known as red blood cell exchange therapy, can reduce the number of sickle cells. In this treatment, a person's blood is drawn, the red blood cells are removed, and those cells are replaced with healthy red blood cells from a donor.

For a successful transfusion, the donated blood must be a blood type match, and it must contain the correct antiantibodies. If a person gets blood from a donor whose blood is not a good match, the person's blood might make antibodies to attack this new blood. An antiantibody is a protein that attacks other antibodies. It can stop an antibody from attacking blood that the antibody thinks is an enemy invader.

Medications

Over-the-counter and prescription painkillers are the most common medications taken by people with sickle cell disease. Antibiotics are also important to prevent and treat infections. As soon as babies are diagnosed with sickle cell, they begin receiving penicillin two times a day to reduce the chance of a severe infection. Regular antibiotics continue until at least age five. Some people may need to take antibiotics throughout their entire lives.

In 1998, hydroxyurea became the first medication approved in the United States to reduce pain crises. Hydroxyurea is an oral medication that increases the amount of fetal hemoglobin, which provides some protection against the effects of sickle hemoglobin. Studies have shown that hydroxyurea reduces instances of pain crises, acute chest syndrome, and severe anemia. It also reduces related hospital visits by 50 percent.[4] At first hydroxyurea was approved for adult patients only. Later studies, however, showed that the medication was safe and effective in children as young as nine months. The medication has not been proven safe for babies under nine months of age. Most experts recommend that children and adults who experience severe pain crises, acute chest syndrome, or anemia take hydroxyurea every day.

The use of hydroxyurea can reduce the total health-care costs of sickle cell disease. A CDC study analyzed health-care costs for children one to three years of age who were taking the medication compared to children who were not receiving it. Children on hydroxyurea had approximately 30 percent fewer hospital stays than those not taking it. The average annual hospital cost for children on the medication was $9,450, a savings of more than $4,000 when compared with that of the children not on the medication.[5]

Bone Marrow

Bone marrow is spongy tissue inside some bones, including hip and thigh bones. It contains immature cells known as stem cells. Some stem cells are pluripotent. This means that they have the potential to become many types of cells, depending on what the body needs. For example, imagine a bad cut that gets dirty. Bone marrow will release stem cells that become white blood cells to fight infection and platelets to help with clotting. As red blood cells reach the end of their lives, bone marrow releases stem cells that become new red blood cells to replace the old ones. Healthy bone marrow produces 200 billion new red blood cells every day.[6]

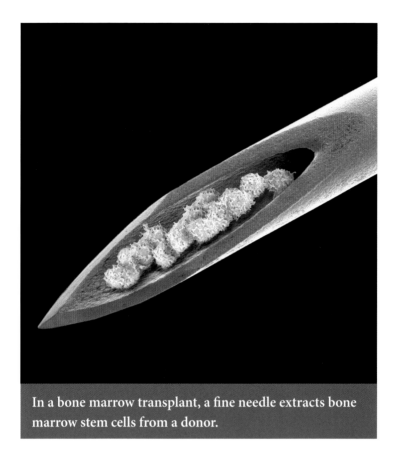

In a bone marrow transplant, a fine needle extracts bone marrow stem cells from a donor.

Cure

The only known cure for sickle cell disease is a blood and bone marrow transplant, also called a stem cell transplant. First the patient receives a course of chemotherapy to kill the bone marrow that is producing abnormal hemoglobin. Next, the patient receives healthy bone marrow stem cells from a donor. The new marrow produces healthy hemoglobin that replaces the abnormal hemoglobin

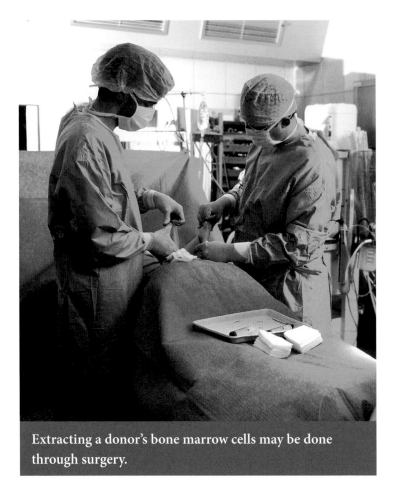

Extracting a donor's bone marrow cells may be done through surgery.

that produces sickle cells. If the transplant if successful, the patient is cured.

However, only a small number of people with sickle cell disease are candidates for a transplant. The patient must be otherwise healthy enough to undergo the procedure. The chemotherapy and the procedure can be risky for some patients, particularly adults with sickle cell disease who have suffered significant organ damage. Patients undergoing a transplant must receive donor bone marrow that is a very good match or else the body will reject the new bone marrow. The best match is a sibling who does not have the trait for sickle cell disease. Most transplants are performed in children who are still relatively healthy.

"One problem with bone marrow transplants is that you need to have a family member whose genes match."[7]

—Dr. Griffin Rodgers, National Institutes of Health

Donating Healthy Cells

Once a sibling is identified as a stem cell donor, the next step is to collect the healthy bone marrow stem cells. This process is called stem cell harvest. Cells are generally collected from the donor's blood by drawing blood from a vein. The blood runs through a special machine. The machine collects the stem cells from the donor's blood, then puts the blood back into the donor. The donor is given medicine to ensure that new stem cells are produced to replace the ones that are removed. The recipient is then able to produce healthy blood cells. Currently only full siblings can donate stem cells to a sibling for transplant in sickle cell disease. Scientists are conducting research that may allow other relatives or even nonrelatives to match as a donor.

Living with Sickle Cell Disease

People living with sickle cell disease can lead full lives, enjoy a range of activities, and accomplish their goals. The disease does, however, impact people's lives. The extent of impact varies from person to person, depending on the severity of their symptoms and complications.

People living with sickle cell disease often tire easily due to persistent anemia, which can limit their ability to be as active and productive as they'd like. Ongoing pain, too, can make it harder to participate in sports and other physical activities. Pain also can make it hard to concentrate. Sickle cell pain episodes and other health crises can require doctor's visits and hospital stays. The result is missed days of work,

With treatment and management, people with sickle cell can enjoy everyday activities with friends.

Academic Accommodations

Schools and colleges consider sickle cell disease a disability and so must offer reasonable changes, or accommodations, to help students with the condition succeed. These accommodations may be both academic and nonacademic. Academic accommodations may include extending time for completing homework or allowing a test to be made up if the student has missed school due to a pain crisis or other health issue. Nonacademic accommodations can help prevent sickle cell episodes. For example, students may need to have the temperature regulated in a classroom or dorm room or have more frequent breaks during physical activity. The most important thing is to maintain communication with teachers and the school.

school, and other activities. Students with sickle cell disease often report feeling like they are always behind at school and must work extra hard to catch up on missed schoolwork.

In addition, people with sickle cell disease sometimes find that teachers, employers, and even health-care workers do not recognize the severity of the disease. This is because symptoms, such as pain crises, come and go and aren't clearly visible. People with sickle cell disease learn how to manage their symptoms, adopt a healthy lifestyle, and take responsibility for their health to live the best life possible.

Healthy Lifestyle

Many symptoms and complications are out of the control of people with sickle cell disease, and medications and medical interventions will remain an important part of managing the disease. Adopting a healthy lifestyle and avoiding known triggers for pain crises, however, allows people living with sickle cell disease to take some level of control. It can help to reduce or prevent pain crises and their long-term effects.

People living with sickle cell disease should avoid overexertion and dehydration, both of which can be pain crisis triggers. That means taking time to rest during physical activity and drinking plenty of fluids. Fluids help the blood flow, which can help prevent some blockages. A balanced diet with plenty of fresh fruits and vegetables is also important. Healthful foods are rich in nutrients that improve hemoglobin levels. Most fresh fruits contain antioxidants, which

"I'm only a patient when I'm in the doctor's office. I'm really a whole person living an active life; I just happen to live with sickle cell disease."[1]

—Tiffany McCoy, a person with sickle cell

help control cell destruction and death, which is a complication of sickle cell disease. Getting a good night's sleep also helps prevent fatigue, which can trigger an episode. Avoiding caffeine, alcohol, and nicotine can help minimize triggers.

Exercise is an important part of a healthy lifestyle. Regular exercise has many health benefits for everyone, including people living with sickle cell disease. It strengthens the heart, lung, and blood vessels. It increases muscle strength and flexibility, which can be affected by sickle cell disease. Regular exercise can increase energy, improve sleep, and combat depression and anxiety. It can reduce the risk of persistent infections and illness. Physical activity

As with anyone, taking breaks to rest and hydrate is important for people with sickle cell disease.

can even function as a natural painkiller. It increases the release of endorphins in the body's nervous system, which can help control pain.

People living with sickle cell disease should remain active, but they may have to modify or avoid some sports. Because sickle cell disease can result in damage to joints and bones, high-impact sports, such as track or gymnastics, may not be recommended. Contact sports such as soccer, football, and hockey also may not be suitable for everyone with sickle cell disease. Sports such as swimming, golf, and skating

Low-impact forms of exercise, such as cycling, are good choices for people with sickle cell.

are excellent aerobic workouts and may be easier on bones and joints. Other physical activities that may be a good choice include walking, cycling, dancing, and gardening. It's a good idea for people with sickle cell disease to talk with their doctor before engaging in a strenuous sport or activity.

Extreme temperatures are pain triggers, so it's important to avoid both extreme hot and cold whenever possible, as well as abrupt changes in temperature. This can be as simple as staying indoors on very hot or cold days. People may want to ease slowly into a swimming pool or lake rather than jumping in.

Taking Responsibility

As people with sickle cell disease grow up and live on their own, they must eventually learn how to take full responsibility for their health care. This process is known in the sickle cell community as transition, and it generally takes place during the teenage years or as a young adult. One of the first steps often is transferring care from a pediatric doctor, who specializes in children, to a doctor who focuses on treating adults. Transition can be a challenging time,

Mental Health

Living with sickle cell disease can be difficult and stressful. People with the disease should pay attention to their mental health in addition to their physical health. They should not hesitate to ask for help when needed. Deep breathing, mindfulness practices, and yoga can help manage stress. Physical activity is a great way to relax tense muscles and lift mood. Family and friends can help relieve stress and anxiety. A patient support group can provide tips and advice to help adjust to living with sickle cell disease. Plus, it's nice to talk with others who understand. If feelings of sadness or anxiety about the disease are interfering with a person's ability to function fully, their doctor may recommend medications or other treatments to improve their quality of life.

and it can be complicated by the fact that it often coincides with major life changes, such as attending college or starting a job, which may involve moving to a new home or city.

During transition, teens and young adults learn to work with their health-care providers to schedule appointments and follow up with any questions they

Moving out and living alone means people with sickle cell need to be equipped to manage the disease independently.

may have for the doctor. It's a time to learn about managing health records, ordering prescriptions, and understanding health insurance. Most importantly, it's a time for young people with sickle cell disease to learn how to advocate for themselves to ensure that they are receiving the best possible care.

"As I got older, I became more knowledgeable and began to take my life and health into my own hands."[2]

—Lance, a person living with sickle cell disease

Hospital Time

Most people living with sickle cell disease become quite skilled at preventing and managing pain and other symptoms at home. They also learn to recognize when it's time to seek medical help. When pain becomes too severe to manage at home, the individual should go to the hospital or emergency room for stronger painkillers and fluids that may need to be given by IV. Any fever higher than 101 degrees Fahrenheit (38°C) is considered a medical emergency due to the risk of serious infections among people with sickle cell disease. Symptoms of acute chest syndrome—such as chest pain, shortness of breath, fever, and increasing fatigue that may signal severe anemia—should prompt a visit to the doctor right away. In addition, unusual headaches, sudden weakness or loss of feeling, or abrupt vision change may be signs of stroke and should be assessed by a doctor immediately.

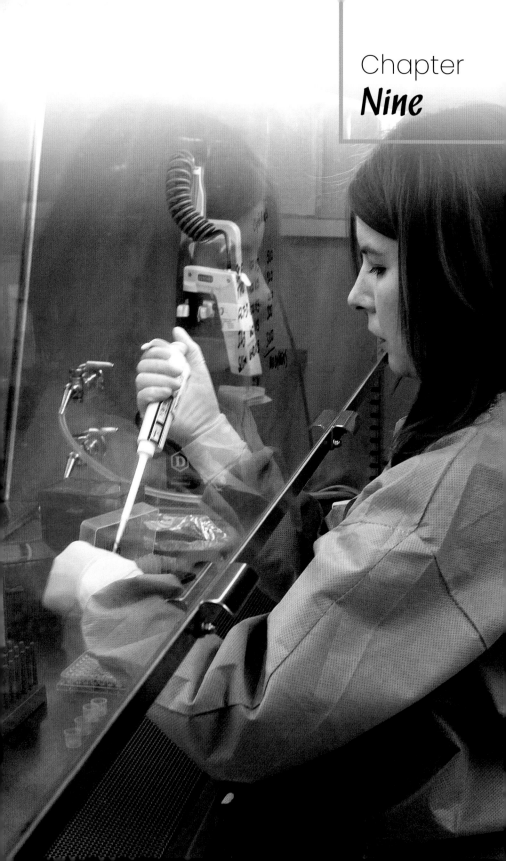

Sickle Cell Research

A number of promising advancements in sickle cell treatment are on the horizon. Researchers say this forward momentum is due to advances in genetic sequencing and a better understanding of the biology of the disease combined with new funding sources. For example, federal funding changes have made it more financially rewarding for drug companies to develop treatments for relatively rare diseases. And in 2019, the National Institutes of Health (NIH) announced plans to spend at least $100 million over the following four years to develop affordable, gene-based cures for sickle cell disease and human immunodeficiency virus (HIV).[1]

Scientists are exploring gene therapy as they work to improve the treatment and management of sickle cell.

Gene Therapy

Because sickle cell disease is caused by a genetic defect, the most promising universal cure is to fix the gene through gene therapy. Gene therapy is an experimental technique to treat or prevent disease by altering the genes inside the body's cells. To treat sickle cell disease with this technique, a specialist would withdraw some of the patient's red blood cells or bone marrow. Then, in a laboratory setting, the scientist would either correct the genetic mistake that causes sickle cell or turn the abnormal gene off, meaning it would no longer provide its harmful instructions to the body. If the mutated gene is turned off, the body would resume making fetal hemoglobin.

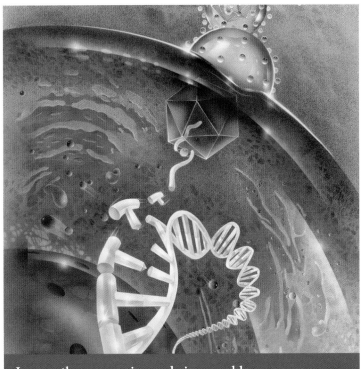

In gene therapy, engineered viruses add new genes, *orange*, to a person's DNA in order to correct a mistake.

An engineered virus then would carry the corrected genes to the bone marrow. The bone marrow would begin producing normal hemoglobin. The fixed cells would be reintroduced to the body. Once the new hemoglobin replaced the old, the sickle cells—and the disease—would disappear.

There would be several advantages to gene therapy as a cure over bone marrow transplant. First, it would use the patient's own bone marrow, so finding a donor match would no longer be an obstacle

How Gene Therapy Works

Ever since scientists recognized that defective genes can make people sick, they have been working on ways to fix or replace those genes to cure or prevent disease. This treatment is known as gene therapy and can work in any one of several ways. It can be used to replace a gene that is causing problems with one that doesn't, it can add genes to a body that will help it fight the disease, or it can be used to turn off the gene that is causing a medical problem. To introduce the altered genes into cells, scientists use what is called a vector, which is like a vehicle that carries things. Viruses make good vectors, but they normally carry infections into cells. In gene therapy, scientists create, or engineer, viruses that can safely deliver the healthy genes.

to the cure. Second, it would not be necessary to give immunosuppressants. When receiving donor marrow, patients must be put on drugs that suppress their immune response to increase chances of a successful transplant. Any time a patient's immune system is suppressed, the risk for infection and other health conditions increases. In addition, a disease called graft versus host disease, in which immune cells from the donor attack the recipient's tissues, would not be a problem. For these reasons, gene therapy would be a more universal cure than bone marrow transplant.

Still, gene therapy is not without its risks. The patient would need a few days of chemotherapy in order to kill off sickle cells and make room for the new altered cells. Chemotherapy can have numerous side effects, including an increased risk of infection and damage to the heart and lung tissue. Gene therapy is still in the experimental stage. It's not clear yet whether the cure would be permanent, but clinical trials have been encouraging. If gene therapy works as a long-term cure, sickle cell disease would be the first genetic illness to be cured by altering genes.

"The dream is that every child diagnosed with sickle cell disease would be cured with gene therapy right at the beginning."[3]

—Dr. Banu Aygun, associate chief of hematology and the sickle cell disease section head at Northwell's Cohen Children's Medical Center

Research Directions

Researchers continue to study sickle cell disease and seek new and better treatments. All people with sickle cell disease have the same genetic defect, yet the number and severity of their symptoms can vary widely. Some have severe pain crises. Others develop severe damage to kidneys, lungs, brains, and other organs. Still others have mild symptoms. Scientists are conducting research to look for a genetic basis for those differences. That would allow doctors to identify children who are at high risk for developing severe complications. Preventative treatments could then begin early before organ damage starts.

Scientists also are looking into the processes in the body that are involved in producing a pain crisis. They seek to learn more about how pain crises happen. With this information, scientists hope to develop medicines and treatments that are more effective in managing and preventing pain crises.

New Medications

After many years with few medication advancements for people with sickle cell disease, several new medications were approved in 2019. The first is Voxelotor, which is an oral medicine for children 12 years of age and older. It prevents red blood cells from forming the sickle shape and clumping together, which improves the flow of blood and oxygen to tissues and organs. Voxelotor may reduce the breakdown of sickle cells and lower the risk of anemia. Possible side effects are headache, diarrhea, abdominal pain, nausea, fatigue, and fever.

The second is Crizanlizumab-tmca. This medication is given through an IV line and helps

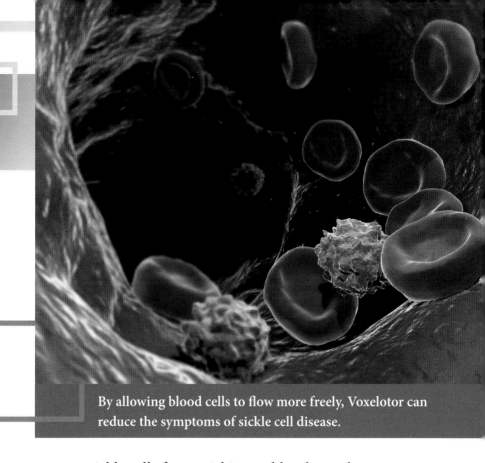

By allowing blood cells to flow more freely, Voxelotor can reduce the symptoms of sickle cell disease.

prevent sickle cells from sticking to blood vessel walls. This reduces inflammation, pain crises, and other complications caused by the blockage of blood flow. Possible side effects are nausea, joint pain, back pain, and fever.

The third approved medication is Adakveo. It blocks a protein called P-selectin that lines the inside of blood vessels and makes them sticky. Blocking this sticky protein means that sickle cells are less likely to get stuck in clumps and block blood flow. Adakveo has been shown to reduce pain crises by 50 percent and may improve overall blood vessel health.

According to Julie Kanter, a hematologist and director of the adult sickle cell center at the University of Alabama School of Medicine, "It's a game changer."[4]

Also approved in 2019 was Oxbryta, a medication for adults and children over 12. It prevents red blood cells from forming the sickle shape and binding together. When Oxbryta was announced in a press release, Beverley Francis-Gibson, president and CEO of the SCDAA, wrote, "After decades of waiting, we now have a treatment option that could change the course of the disease."[5]

These are just some of the latest advances. There are more than 40 different medications being developed to treat different aspects of the disease

Clinical Trials

New drugs and treatments aren't available for patients to use as soon as they're made. First, they need to be studied to make sure that they are safe and helpful. A clinical trial is a type of research that studies the new treatment. These trials must be approved by scientific and ethical authorities before they can start. Patients may choose to participate in a clinical trial. There are risks involved in clinical trials. There may be side effects to the treatment that weren't known, or the treatment may not be as effective as hoped. But there are benefits too. The patient has access to the most current care and is helping develop effective treatments for others.

and dozens of clinical trials underway. The drugs and treatments under investigation involve new ways to reduce or eliminate pain crises, prevent widespread organ damage, and protect the brain from strokes.

Many people living with sickle cell disease are living their lives to the fullest and taking charge of their health care. Newborn screening, daily doses of antibiotics, transfusions, and other medications and therapies already have greatly increased the average life expectancies for people with sickle cell disease and improved their overall well-being. And a small but growing number of people have been cured through bone marrow transplants. With advances in gene therapy and other potential treatments, researchers envision a future in which all people are cured, and sickle cell disease, and its lifetime of pain and organ damage, becomes a thing of the past.

"I want to showcase the fact that you can have [sickle cell disease] but can also do everything else. . . . We can still achieve whatever we want to do, whatever we put our minds to."[6]

—Fatimah, a person living with sickle cell disease

Essential
Facts

Facts about Sickle Cell Disease

- Sickle cell disease is a group of inherited blood disorders that can cause pain, anemia, infection, and other serious health problems.
- Abnormal hemoglobin makes red blood cells become stiff and sickle shaped. The sickle cells form clumps that block blood vessels, depriving cells of blood and oxygen.
- An estimated 100,000 people in the United States live with sickle cell disease, and approximately 2.5 million carry the trait for sickle cell.
- Sickle cell disease is a result of a genetic mutation inherited from both parents.
- Sickle cell disease affects millions worldwide and is most prevalent among people from parts of the world where malaria is or was common.
- Sickle cell disease most likely evolved as a defense against malaria.

How Sickle Cell Disease Affects Daily Life

- Sickle cell disease is a serious and lifelong disease.
- Pain is the most common complication of sickle cell disease and the main reason why people with sickle cell disease go to the hospital.
- Blocked blood vessels in the arms, legs, chest, or abdomen can cause severe pain, called a sickle cell episode or a pain crisis.
- People living with sickle cell disease can work to avoid pain crisis triggers, which include extreme temperatures, dehydration, overexertion, and infection.

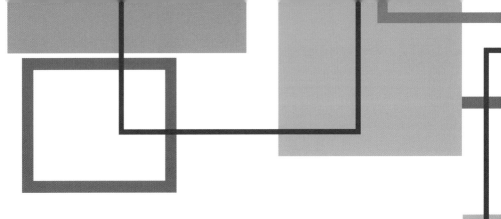

- Repeatedly blocked blood vessels can cause damage to the joints, lungs, kidneys, brain, and other organs.
- Anemia is a common complication of sickle cell disease. It is a condition caused by a lack of healthy red blood cells, which results in fatigue and weakness.
- Transition is when young adults living with sickle cell disease take responsibility for their own health care.

How Sickle Cell Disease Can Be Treated and Managed

- All 50 states and the District of Columbia screen newborns for sickle cell disease so treatment can begin early.
- Children are prescribed daily antibiotics to prevent infections.
- The most common treatments for sickle cell disease include painkillers, antibiotics, and blood transfusions.
- The only known cure for sickle cell disease is a bone marrow or stem cell transplant.
- Scientists are testing gene therapies that offer promising potential cures for sickle cell disease.
- A healthy lifestyle can reduce or prevent pain crises. People living with sickle cell disease should drink plenty of fluids, eat a well-balanced diet, and get plenty of rest and sleep.

Quote

"I'm only a patient when I'm in the doctor's office. I'm really a whole person living an active life; I just happen to live with sickle cell disease."

—Tiffany McCoy, a person with sickle cell disease

Glossary

acute
Strong and often short-lived.

antibody
A protein that the immune system uses to fight infection.

artery
A large blood vessel that carries blood from the heart to the rest of the body.

chemotherapy
The use of chemicals to kill diseased cells, often with severe side effects.

chronic
Continuing for a long time.

diagnosis
The identification of an illness in a person by a medical professional.

fatigue
Extreme tiredness.

intravenous (IV)
Happening within or entering through a vein.

lethargic
Tired and slow.

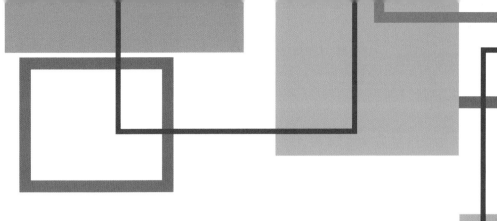

nutrient

A mineral that is absorbed by the roots of plants or digestive systems of animals for nourishment.

plasma

The clear, yellow, liquid part of the blood.

platelet

A disk-shaped cell found in the blood that is involved in clotting.

prevalence

How widely present something is.

protein

An amino acid chain present in organic material, such as skin, hair, or blood.

vector

A virus or fragment of DNA that carries foreign genetic material into cells.

Additional
Resources

Selected Bibliography

"A Century of Progress: Milestones in Sickle Cell Disease Research and Care." *National Heart, Lung, and Blood Institute*, n.d., nhlbi.nih.gov. Accessed 6 Mar. 2020.

Harrington, Joy. "New Hope for a Sickle Cell Cure." *Sickle Cell Disease Association of America*, 2 Dec. 2019, sicklecelldisease.org. Accessed 6 Mar. 2020.

"Sickle Cell Disease (SCD)." *Centers for Disease Control and Prevention*, 21 Oct. 2019, cdc.gov. Accessed 6 Mar. 2020.

Further Readings

Allman, Toney. *Genetics and Medicine*. ReferencePoint, 2018.

Mooney, Carla. *How Genetic Research Changed the World*. ReferencePoint, 2019.

Morris, Alexandra. *Medical Research and Technology*. Abdo, 2016.

Online Resources

Booklinks
NONFICTION NETWORK
FREE! ONLINE NONFICTION RESOURCES

To learn more about handling sickle cell disease, please visit **abdobooklinks.com** or scan this QR code. These links are routinely monitored and updated to provide the most current information available.

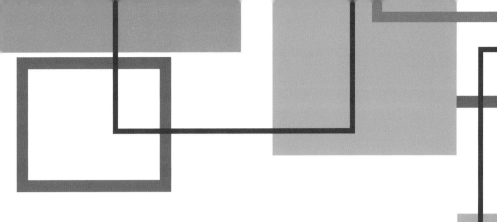

More Information

For more information on this subject, contact or visit the following organizations:

American Sickle Cell Anemia Association

DD Bldg. at the Cleveland Clinic, Ste. DD1-201
10900 Carnegie Ave.
Cleveland, OH 44106
216-229-8600
ascaa.org

The American Sickle Cell Anemia Association is a nonprofit organization that provides a wide range of services to individuals and families with sickle cell disease and sickle cell trait. Its website includes information on programs and services, upcoming events, and answers to frequently asked questions.

Sickle Cell Disease Association of America

7240 Parkway Dr., Ste. 180
Hanover, MD 21076
410-528-1555
sicklecelldisease.org

The website of the Sickle Cell Disease Association of America includes information, news, research, and resources on sickle cell disease. It also includes an interactive state map to access SCDAA chapters.

Source Notes

CHAPTER 1. WHAT IS SICKLE CELL DISEASE?

1. "Real Stories." *CDC*, 21 Oct. 2019, cdc.gov. Accessed 6 Mar. 2020.

2. "A Century of Progress: Milestones in Sickle Cell Disease Research and Care." *U.S. Department of Health and Human Services*, Sept. 2010, nhlbi.nih.gov. Accessed 18 Aug. 2020.

3. "A Century of Progress."

CHAPTER 2. THE CAUSE

1. "Sickle Cell Disease." *NIH*, 17 Aug. 2020, ghr.nlm.nih.gov. Accessed 18 Aug. 2020.

2. "Frequently Asked Questions Regarding Sickle Cell Trait." *American Society of Hematology*, 25 Jan. 2012, hematology.org. Accessed 18 Aug. 2020.

3. Katie Langin. "Sickle Cell Anemia Traced Back to One Baby Born 7300 Years Ago." *Science*, 9 Mar. 2018, sciencemag.org. Accessed 18 Aug. 2020.

CHAPTER 3. SICKLE CELL DEMOGRAPHICS

1. "Sickle Cell Disease." *WHO*, 2020, afro.who.int. Accessed 18 Aug. 2020.

2. Joseph E. Maakaron. "What Is the Global Prevalence of Sickle Cell Disease (SCD)?" *Medscape*, 4 Aug. 2020, medscape.com. Accessed 18 Aug. 2020.

3. "Questions and Answers about Sickle Cell Trait." *NIH*, 22 Sept. 2010, nhlbi.nih.gov. Accessed 18 Aug. 2020.

4. Sarah Boseley. "Malaria Kills Twice As Many People As Previously Thought, Research Finds." *Guardian*, 2 Feb. 2012, theguardian.com. Accessed 18 Aug. 2020.

5. "Data & Statistics." *CDC*, 21 Oct. 2019, cdc.gov. Accessed 18 Aug. 2020.

6. "About Sickle Cell Disease." *NIH*, 26 May 2020, genome.gov. Accessed 18 Aug. 2020.

7. Karen Weintraub. "Time Has Finally Come for Sickle Cell Advancements." *WebMD*, 26 Nov. 2019, webmd.com. Accessed 21 Mar. 2020.

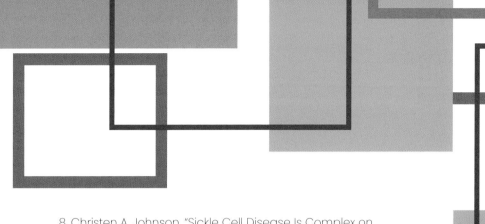

8. Christen A. Johnson. "Sickle Cell Disease Is Complex on Its Own, but Black Men with the Illness Battle Its Stigmas and Stereotypes Too." *Medical Xpress*, 31 Dec. 2019, medicalxpress.com. Accessed 18 Aug. 2020.

9. "Sickle Cell Disease (SCD) in California, 2016." *CDC*, n.d., cdc.gov. Accessed 18 Aug. 2020.

10. Jenny Gold. "Sickle Cell Patients Endure Discrimination, Poor Care and Shortened Lives." *NPR*, 4 Nov. 2017, npr.org. Accessed 18 Aug. 2020.

11. "Data & Statistics on Sickle Cell Disease." *CDC*, 21 Oct. 2019, cdc.gov. Accessed 18 Aug. 2020.

12. Emad Yanni et al. "Trends in Pediatric Sickle Cell Disease-Related Mortality in the United States, 1983-2002." *Journal of Pediatrics*, 1 Apr. 2009, jpeds.com. Accessed 18 Aug. 2020.

13. Deborah Lubeck et al. "Estimated Life Expectancy and Income of Patients with Sickle Cell Disease Compared with Those without Sickle Cell Disease." *JAMA Network*, 15 Nov. 2019, jamanetwork.com. Accessed 18 Aug. 2020.

14. J. Huo et al. "The Economic Burden of Sickle Cell Disease in the United States." *Value in Health*, 1 Sept. 2018, valueinhealthjournal.com. Accessed 18 Aug. 2020.

CHAPTER 4. DIAGNOSING SICKLE CELL DISEASE

1. "Real Stories." *CDC*, 21 Oct. 2019, cdc.gov. Accessed 6 Mar. 2020.

2. "Newborn Screening 101." *Baby's First Test*, 2020, babysfirsttest.org. Accessed 18 Aug. 2020.

3. "Improving Sickle Cell Care in the U.S. and Abroad." *Children's Hospital of Philadelphia*, 12 Mar. 2013, research.chop.edu. Accessed 18 Aug. 2020.

Source Notes
Continued

CHAPTER 5. PAIN CRISES

1. "From Africa to the U.S.: A Young Woman's Search for Sickle Cell Disease Treatment." *NIH*, 15 Jan. 2020, magazine.medlineplus.gov. Accessed 6 Mar. 2020.

2. Roni Caryn Rabin. "Easing the Pain of Sickle Cell Disease." *New York Times*, 20 Oct. 2014, well.blogs.nytimes.com. Accessed 18 Aug. 2020.

3. Joy Harrington. "New Hope for a Sickle Cell Cure." *Sickle Cell Disease Association of America*, 2 Dec. 2019, sicklecelldisease.org. Accessed 6 Mar. 2020.

CHAPTER 6. SICKLE CELL DISEASE AND HEALTH

1. "Sickle Cell Disease." *NIH*, 1 Mar. 2020, nhlbi.nih.gov. Accessed 6 Mar. 2020.

2. "Sickle Cell Disease." *CDC*, 21 Oct. 2019, cdc.gov. Accessed 6 Mar. 2020.

3. "Sickle Cell Disease," *CDC*.

4. Fenwick T Nichols III. "Stroke Associated with Sickle Cell Disease." *MedLink*, 3 June 2020, medlink.com. Accessed 18 Aug. 2020.

CHAPTER 7. TREATMENT AND MANAGEMENT

1. "Are Family Physicians Comfortable Treating People with Sickle Cell Disease?" *CDC*, 21 Oct. 2019, cdc.gov. Accessed 18 Aug. 2020.

2. "A Century of Progress: Milestones in Sickle Cell Disease Research and Care." *U.S. Department of Health and Human Services*, Sept. 2010, nhlbi.nih.gov. Accessed 18 Aug. 2020.

3. "A Century of Progress."

4. "Sickle Cell Disease Research & Care." *NIH*, 12 Apr. 2012, nhlbi.nih.gov. Accessed 18 Aug. 2020.

5. "Is Hydroxyurea Treatment Associated with Lower Medical Costs for Young Children with Sickle Cell Anemia?" *CDC*, 21 Oct. 2019, cdc.gov. Accessed 18 Aug. 2020.

6. Hannah Nichols. "All You Need to Know about Bone Marrow." *Medical News Today*, 15 Dec. 2017, medicalnewstoday.com. Accessed 18 Aug. 2020.

7. "Updates from NIH's Sickle Cell Disease Scientists." *NIH*, 13 Jan. 2020, magazine.medlineplus.gov. Accessed 6 Mar. 2020.

CHAPTER 8. LIVING WITH SICKLE CELL DISEASE

1. "Real Stories." *CDC*, 21 Oct. 2019, cdc.gov. Accessed 6 Mar. 2020.

2. "Real Stories."

CHAPTER 9. SICKLE CELL RESEARCH

1. "NIH Launches New Collaboration to Develop Gene-Based Cures for Sickle Cell Disease and HIV on Global Scale." *NIH*, 23 Oct. 2019, nhlbi.nih.gov. Accessed 6 Mar. 2020.

2. Jon Cohen and Jocelyn Kaiser. "NIH and Gates Foundation Lay Out Ambitious Plan to Bring Gene-Based Treatments for HIV and Sickle Cell Disease to Africa." *Science*, 23 Oct. 2019, sciencemag.org. Accessed 18 Aug. 2020.

3. Joy Harrington. "New Hope for a Sickle Cell Cure." *Sickle Cell Disease Association of America*, 2 Dec. 2019, sicklecelldisease.org. Accessed 6 Mar. 2020.

4. Karen Weintraub. "Time Has Finally Come for Sickle Cell Advancements." *WebMD*, 26 Nov. 2019, webmd.com. Accessed 21 Mar. 2020.

5. Weintraub, "Time Has Finally Come."

6. "Real Stories." *CDC*, 21 Oct. 2019, cdc.gov. Accessed 6 Mar. 2020.

Index

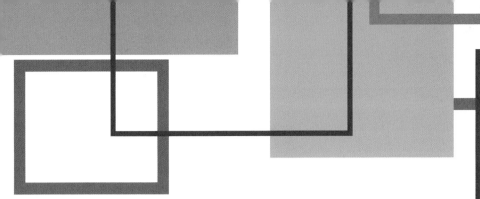

About the
Author

Yvette LaPierre

Yvette LaPierre lives in North Dakota with her family and teaches writing at the University of North Dakota. She writes and edits books and articles for children and adults.

About the Consultant
Tirthadipa Pradhan-Sundd, PhD

Tirthadipa Pradhan-Sundd, PhD, lives in Pittsburgh, Pennsylvania, with her family and is an assistant professor at the University of Pittsburgh School of Medicine. Her research work focuses on how sickle cell disease affects the liver.